Ready for Research

Produced in collaboration with colleagues from the National Institute for Health and Care Research
Clinical Research Network Greater Manchester
Clinical Research Network West Midlands

Emma Oughton | Carly Tibbins | Tilly Bridger-Staatz
Louise Woodhead | Andrea Shilton | Robert Hughes

Published in association with
Bear With Us Productions

ISBN 9798388911155

Brand by Richie Evans
Design by Emma Evans
Illustrated by Novel Varius
www.justbearwithus.com

Written by
Alex Winstanley

Illustrated by
Novel Varius

Do you know about research?
I didn't, but now I do.
Let me tell you a story,
about how research
might help you.

"Yes please!"

I nodded big, and listened as she began to talk. "I ran on a machine in a clinic, and then I had to walk.

A nurse counted my **heartbeat** and listened to my chest.

Then did the tests again — after I'd had some rest."

So I spoke to other people,
about research they'd been in too.
From online forms to test tubes,
research even studies poo!

Research didn't sound scary, in fact it sounded fun! I was amazed by how much it could help each and everyone.

My dad also told me,
"Let me know what you decide,
and if you choose to be involved,
you can always change your mind!"

"I'm ready now,"
I said, showing the leaflet to my dad.
"That's great, let's give consent.
The researchers will be glad!"

On research day we were greeted
by a nurse with a huge smile.
She checked I was still saying yes,
consenting to the trial.

—MENTAL WELLBEING—

My research took a few months,
I enjoyed it — it was fun!
I even made some new friends,
and before I knew it,
it was done!

Then when a friend at school
said that they were scared too,
I told them **all about research.**

"If I can do it,
     then so can you!"

Research is there to help us.
The more we research, the more we know.
We learn to fight pandemics,
or the healthiest foods to grow.

Do **you feel ready** for research?
I hope that now you do.

Thanks for reading my story
about how research might help you.

Quiz Questions

- What age do you have to be to take part in research?

- If a child gives their consent (their permission) to take part in research what is that called ?

- If you say yes to being involved in research, do you have to stay for the whole study?

- Is research only carried out in a hospital?

- Does research only help the person taking part?

Job roles

Who am I ?

- Chief Investigator

- Doctor

- Participant

- Pharmacist

- PPIE member
(Public & Patient Involvement and Engagement)

- Principal Investigator

- Research Nurse

- Research Practitioner

- Researcher

Glossary

- **Assent** – a young person under 16 giving their permission to take part in research.

- **Blinding** – when the person in the trial doesn't know which medicine they are taking or if they are taking the medicine or a placebo.

- **Clinical trial** – a research study that involves testing a medicine, device or intervention.

- **Consent/consent form** – anyone over 16 has to give their permission to take part in research, this is a legal document.

- **Dissemination** – how the findings of the research are shared with others.

- **Ethics** – to make sure the rights and safety of all people involved in research is the most important thing.

- NIHR – National Institute for Health and Care Research –they fund and deliver the research.

- Participant – a person who takes part in the research.

- Placebo – a dummy medication – the control group.

- Questionnaire – a set of questions to find out information.

- Randomisation – a fair way of seeing which group you will be put into for the research.

- Research – to find out an answer to a question.

- Unblinding – when you find out what medicine you were taking.

- Wellbeing – making sure your body and mind is fit and healthy.

Alex Winstanley is a best-selling author and award-winning social entrepreneur. Through his books, he raises awareness of a range of long-term health conditions, in a positive and supportive way, for children and young people. He is extremely passionate about promoting a diverse and inclusive society, where every person is valued and celebrated. His books are inspired by real people, as Alex believes nothing is more important than giving a voice to those with lived experience.

See more of Alex's books and the work of his disabled people's-led social enterprise, Happy Smiles Training, at
www.happysmilestraining.co.uk

Happy Smiles Training is an award-winning disabled people's-led social enterprise. Based in Wigan, they deliver inclusive training to schools, community groups and businesses across the North West and further afield. With over 90% of their team made up of disabled people, their aim is to create inclusive communities for all. Get in touch for more information at **www.happysmilestraining.co.uk**

Be Part of Research is a website run by the National Institute for Health and Care Research (NIHR). It is there to help people find and volunteer for studies happening near where they live.

www.bepartofresearch.nihr.ac.uk

Printed in Great Britain
by Amazon